Print ISBN 978-1-955364-50-8

Vets Publish
www.vetspublish.com

Santa Loves Chess

Written By: Daniel Hallback

Little one, it is time for bed.
Tomorrow is a special day.

Yes, tomorrow is Christmas!

We have to get ready for Santa Claus to visit.

What do we need to do to get ready?

Most people have cookies and a glass of milk for Santa.

People leave Santa milk and cookies so that he can have a snack while he is delivering all of the toys to the children around the world.
I know something else that Santa loves!

What does Santa Love?

Santa Loves Chess!

Santa loves the same game that you and I play?

Yes! Santa loves to play chess at the North Pole. He plays against Mrs Clause, the Elves, and the Reindeer.

I am not sure. I do think that in additional to milk and cookies we should leave Santa a chess puzzle and a note.

That sounds fun, do you think he will do the chess puzzle?

I think that he will, let's make it a mate in one christmas chess puzzle.

Will that be too easy?

We will give Santa a special checkmate in one chess puzzle.
This puzzle will use a special move as part of the answer.

That puzzles looks tough. I do not know the answer or the special move.

It is checkmate in one move, however you have to consider the previous move. After black played their pawn to E5 white can capture the pawn via the special move En Passant. It is as if the pawn only moved forward one square.

I think that he will. He will be very happy that we left him a chess puzzle surprise.

Yes! Hopefully Santa shares the puzzle with his little helpers, the reindeer, and Mrs Clause!

Goodnight, I can't wait for Christmas and seeing if Santa solved the puzzle.

"Merry Christmas To All and To All a Good Knight"